W9-BXA-883

INTRODUCING UNDERWATER ARCHAEOLOGY

25142

The Lerner Archaeology Series

DIGGING UP THE PAST

INTRODUCING UNDERWATER ARCHAEOLOGY

by Elisha Linder and Avner Raban

retold for young readers by Richard L. Currier

 Lerner Publications Company □ Minneapolis

Designed by Ofra Kamar

LIBRARY OF CONGRESS CATALOGING IN PUBLICATION DATA

Currier, Richard L.
Introducing underwater archaeology.

(Digging up the Past: The Lerner Archaeology Series)
Includes index.
SUMMARY: Explains the methods and equipment used by
modern archaeologists and describes some of the discoveries
these scientists have made in oceans throughout the world.

1. Underwater archaeology—Juvenile literature. [Under-
water archaeology. 2. Archaeology] I. **Linder, Elisha**, and
Raban, Avner, authors. Introducing underwater archaeology.
II. Title.

CC77.U5C87 1976   930′.1′02804   72-10801
ISBN 0-8225-0834-6

*This book is also cataloged under the names of Elisha Linder
and Avner Raban.*

First published in the United States of America 1976
by Lerner Publications Company, Minneapolis, Minnesota.

Copyright © 1976 by G. A. The Jerusalem Publishing House.
39, Tchernechovski St., P. O. B. 7147, Jerusalem.

All rights reserved. No part of this publication may be reproduced, stored in a retrieval system
or transmitted, in any form or by any means, electronic, mechanical, photocopying, recording or
otherwise, without the prior permission of the copyright owner.

International Standard Book Number: 0-8225-0834-6
Library of Congress Catalog Card Number: 72-10801

Manufactured in the United States.

CONTENTS

I   ARCHAEOLOGY UNDER WATER

Archaeology is the science of finding, collecting, preserving, and studying objects that have survived from ancient times. Most archaeologists either dig in the earth for these objects or find them in the ruins of ancient houses, palaces, temples, and fortresses. Archaeologists have discovered and explored some of the famous ruins of ancient civilizations, such as the pyramids of Egypt and the great temples of the Aztecs in Mexico and the Incas in South America. They have also studied many ancient mysteries, such as the strange stone formations of Stonehenge in England or the great stone heads of Easter Island.

Archaeology is only about 100 years old—fairly young as sciences go. But there is a special branch of archaeology that is younger still, and that did not really become important until almost the middle of this century. This is the science called "underwater archaeology."

Underwater archaeology is the science of finding, collecting, preserving, and studying ancient objects that have become lost or buried under water. Occasionally, these ancient remains are found in freshwater lakes. Some of the oldest intact remains of wooden ships and houses, for example, have been recovered from the bottoms of certain lakes in northern Europe. Usually, however, ancient remains are found beneath the sea—near harbors, at the bottoms of bays or inlets, or along important sea routes. In order to uncover these remains, underwater archaeologists make use of special kinds of tools. Most archaeologists use picks, shovels, brooms, and brushes in their work, but underwater archaeologists use submarines, aqualungs, diving masks, and other kinds of underwater equipment. Underwater archaeology is, in most respects, a very new and very different kind of archaeology.

In this book we will take a look at

A diver holding a pottery vessel found in the harbor of Atlit, an ancient Phoenician city located in present-day Israel

the kinds of underwater explorations that this new breed of archaeologists carries out. We will also look at the methods that underwater archaeologists use to locate and bring up ancient objects and at some of the more interesting remains that have been discovered and explored under the waters of oceans, bays, harbors, and lakes.

The work of the underwater archaeologists may sound glamorous and romantic, and in fact it *is* one of the most exciting of all scientific jobs. But it is important to remember that, in addition to the many years of training and study required, there is much that is tedious and painstaking in the work of underwater archaeologists. The area of an ancient ruin must be mapped carefully and precisely, the objects must be moved with great care (since they are often so fragile and corroded that they crumble easily), and the exact location of every object the archaeologists find must be recorded. And this is only the beginning. Once the objects are brought back to the universities and museums where these archaeologists work, each piece must be carefully cleaned, labelled, photographed, and studied.

There is no doubt that the underwater archaeologist has one of the most difficult jobs of any modern scientist. His work is often dangerous, and his working conditions are uncomfortable and physically exhausting. It is not easy to find objects — even large ones — that have been lying on the sea bottom for hundreds or even thousands of years. But we should also remember that those very obstacles that make life difficult for the underwater archaeologist have served to preserve the remains of the ancient past.

The archaeologist who works on land is not so lucky. Ancient objects that have fallen to the ground can be picked up and carried off by a curious passer-by. Even if they are left where they fall, they are usually soon destroyed by the elements. Objects of wood, leather, cloth, paper, and other organic materials quickly rot and return to the soil, while objects of metal gradually rust and corrode, leaving nothing but a stain in the earth. The sea, however, can act as a natural preservative.

The saltiness of the sea inhibits the growth of bacteria, and objects made of wood or leather can actually be pickled in the salty brine of the oceans. And while it is true that most metals corrode very rapidly near the seashore because the salty dampness of the air speeds up the

Above: A diver mapping an underwater ruin

Left: This diver is making accurate measurements of underwater finds with the aid of a device called a "level."

Below: A diver makes an archaeological survey using a "hydrodynamic cradle." (See the text on pp. 24–25.)

chemical breakdown of the metal, conditions are quite different on the sea bottom. It is wet and salty down there, but there is not much air. And it is the oxygen in the air that rusts and corrodes metal, not the salt or the water. This is why ancient objects made of metal are sometimes in excellent condition even after they have been under water for hundreds of years. Buried in the nearly airless mud of the sea bottom, they have actually been protected from rust and corrosion. Had they been on land, many of these objects might have been lost to science many generations ago.

What Kinds of Remains Can Be Found in the Sea?

Underwater archaeologists usually find two very different kinds of objects in the sea. On the one hand, they find the ruined remains of

Archaeologists examine a Bronze-Age anchor found on the ocean floor. The stone anchor is carved with an image of a ship's rudder.

ancient villages and harbors that for some reason have sunk beneath the surface of the water. On the other hand, archaeologists find the remains of ships and their cargoes that sank to the bottom when a storm, a battle, or a fire at sea destroyed the vessels. The problems that the archaeologists face and the things they look for depend on which of these two basic types of underwater ruins they are going to explore and investigate.

One of the general problems facing underwater archaeologists is that of dating the remains they find. In the case of the remains of villages and harbors, it is often difficult to tell how old the ruins are. Did a certain ruin sink beneath the water while people were still living in it, or had it been abandoned first? If it *had* been abandoned, had it been empty for just a few years or for many hundreds of years before it

Small objects found on the muddy bottom of the sea

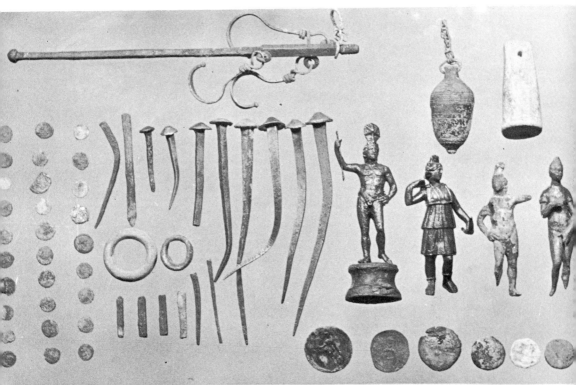

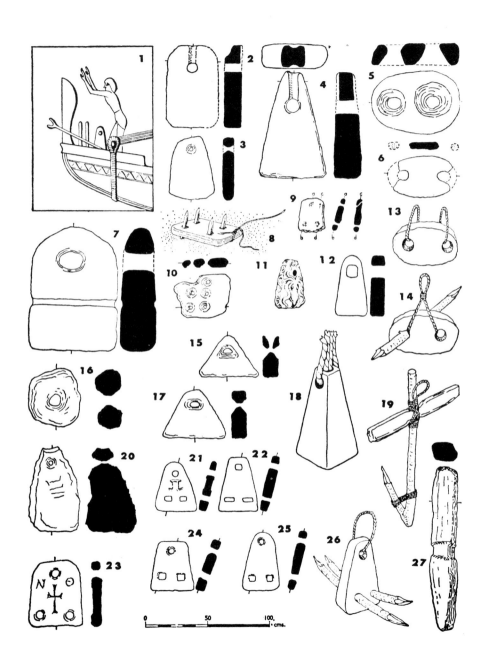

sank? How long has it been under water? Such questions may be very difficult to answer.

If the remains are the result of a shipwreck, it may be easier to determine their age, because we can assume that, on a certain day, a disaster occurred. Perhaps a ship was caught in a storm or destroyed by gunfire. Perhaps it was in danger of running aground, and its frightened crew tossed some of its cargo overboard to lighten the load. There may be a record of the event somewhere, either on land or in the shipwreck itself.

Shipwrecks can sometimes be dated by the dates found on coins in the wreck. Here is the way this method of dating works. Suppose you found an old cash register in an abandoned store. Looking inside the cash drawer, suppose you found a lot of old coins still lying there. Now suppose you wrote down the dates on all the coins, and you found that the oldest coin was dated 1885 and the youngest was dated 1922. You would know for sure that the store could not have been abandoned before 1922. Otherwise, how could a 1922 coin have gotten into the cash register? And if you also found coins from 1921, 1920, 1919, and 1918, you could make a reasonable guess that the store had been abandoned soon after 1922, since otherwise there would probably have been coins from after 1922 as well. Therefore, if you know that the store was not abandoned *before* 1922, and you also know that it could not have been abandoned much *after* 1922, you can be fairly sure that the store was abandoned either in 1922 or soon afterward.

Left: This drawing shows some of the many kinds of anchors used by the seafarers of the ancient world. Underwater archaeologists sometimes use anchors as a means of dating remains found in the sea. These scientists have studied the development of the anchor in ancient times and can determine the age of certain types of anchors by means of their shapes and the materials out of which they are made. They know, for instance, that stone anchors with one hole and with a groove at the top for a rope (Figures 2 and 4) are very ancient, dating from around the 20th century B.C. Stone anchors with three holes (Figures 21, 22, 24, and 25) come from a much later period—the 4th to the 6th centuries B.C. When archaeologists find one of these familiar kinds of anchors associated with a wrecked ship, they can use it to establish the relative age of the ruin.

Pottery can also be used in dating ruins found under the sea. Each of the pottery vessels pictured above comes from a different period of ancient history: 1) 14th century BC.; 2) 10th century B.C.; 3–4) 5th century B.C.; 5) 3rd century B.C.; 6–7) 2nd century B.C.; 8) 6th century A.D. Shipwrecks with similar pieces of pottery in their cargos probably date from the same historical periods.

Archaeologists use this same basic method in fixing the year of a shipwreck by means of the coins on board at the time the ship went down.

A different problem in dating arises when archaeologists find underwater remains that have been washed away by a river current or a strong tide and deposited some distance from their original location. This happens quite often during floods and violent storms, but un-

fortunately the rather mangled remains that result from these natural disasters are not of great scientific value to the archaeologist. The problem is that such objects have become separated from the other materials that might give clues as to their age and origin.

It is usually impossible to be certain about the age of an ancient object unless it can be connected with several other objects, such as a ruined city, an ancient temple, or a bag of coins. When archaeologists know the age of one thing in a certain ruin—whether that thing is a house, a coin, a throne, a coffin, or a book—they can often assign ages to the other objects found together with it. But when a single object has been washed away by a raging flood or a powerful tide, there is little chance that its age can be determined with any accuracy at all. Then the archaeologist can only guess, and scientists hate guesses!

How the Sea Preserves, Conceals— and Destroys

The fate of an object that falls into the sea depends upon *where* it falls. In some places it will be destroyed in a matter of days or weeks, while in other places it may be preserved for centuries almost without damage.

If something falls into the ocean near the shore, it will soon be ground or smashed to bits by the action of the waves. This will happen even if the object falls into fairly deep water, because the action of the waves is felt quite a distance below the surface. Waves that are two feet high exert a grinding action on the objects below them down to a depth of 10 feet. The much larger waves of the ocean are capable of destroying objects on the bottom to depths of 50 feet or more.

Even when an object sinks into the water deep enough to protect it from the action of waves on the surface, it still may not be safe. If the sea bottom where it sinks is covered only with rocks and pebbles, then the object will just lie on the rough surface, where it can be damaged or destroyed by a combination of two destructive forces. The first of these is the action of the water itself. Even at tremendous depths, the waters of the seas and oceans are moving, flowing with tides and currents that may not be particularly fierce but can still erode and destroy things that are exposed to them year after year.

The second destructive force comes from the living creatures of the sea. Plants and animals will attach themselves to the surface of almost any submerged object, even the bottom of a ship. Some of these living creatures may burrow inside certain objects, either to eat them or simply to look for safe homes. Imagine what your favorite possession would look like if you dropped it in the sea, and it was crawled over and chewed on by snails and octopuses or covered with creatures such as barnacles, who cemented their crusty bodies all over its surface. Imagine its condition after it was invaded by worms and other animals who drilled holes through it, hollowed out little spaces inside it, or even ate parts of it—and then was dragged back and forth by tides and currents over a bed of rocks and pebbles for about 10 years!

On the other hand, an object may sink into deep layers of mud and ooze and simply disappear from sight. No tides or currents can harm it when it is safely hidden in the soft, dark blanket of slime and muck, which may keep and preserve it for centuries. In such sea bottoms, archaeologists often find objects that would have been destroyed in a few generations if they had been left on land, yet they may be in nearly perfect condition after a thousand years or more under water!

For instance, ancient ships have been found in a complete state of preservation on the bottom of the sea, with their wooden parts, ropes, masts, metal nails, and cargoes—even including articles made of reeds, leather, or cloth—all intact. Of course, the ship itself is no longer shaped quite like a ship after all this time. The weight of the ship itself and the cargo it carried gradually flattens the sides of the ship outwards, until it sprawls like a pancake on the bottom of the sea.

Although the flattened ship may not make an especially pretty picture for underwater photographers, its collapse helps to preserve it. Once the various parts of the ship are all lying flat on the bottom, they may become covered with sand and mud and thus protected from the destruction caused by waves, currents, and sea animals.

If the sea bottom is rocky, the wooden parts of the shipwrecks quickly disappear, except perhaps for some objects that may have become buried under the ship's cargo. Objects made of metal will rust and corrode, perhaps not as fast as they would on land, but still quickly enough to disappear completely as the years pass.

Sometimes a sunken object lying exposed on the bottom of the sea will become covered with great numbers of tiny sea animals. As time passes, layer after layer of these animals may grow on the object's surface, until it is no longer possible to tell what it originally was. Meanwhile, the object itself may be disintegrating and decomposing inside its cocoon of chalky coral or barnacle shells. If the object is made of metal, it may eventually rust away completely,

On the left is a clay figurine encrusted with small marine animals. The same figurine is shown on the right after having been cleaned.

leaving only a hollow space inside the mass of encrusted animal material. When archaeologists cut open shapeless chalky blocks like these, they often discover a hollow place inside in the shape of a nail, an axe blade, a rifle barrel, or a sword.

In a ruin on the shores of the Mediterranean Sea, in what is now the state of Israel, divers once found several swords that were encrusted with a thick, chalky deposit. From the general size and shape of the remains, archaeologists knew that the swords had once belonged to the Crusaders, European knights who tried to take the Holy Land away from its Moslem rulers during the Middle Ages. The Crusader swords were so completely deteriorated that it was impossible to chip off the encrustation and be left with anything at all. But the archaeologists hit upon the idea of x-raying the finds. The x-rays revealed clear pictures of the old swords hidden under the heavy encrustation.

The manner in which objects become encrusted with sea life is often affected by the temperature of the surrounding water. In the cool waters of the northwestern Mediterranean, for example, the process of encrustation is comparatively slow, while in the warm waters of the Red Sea, small marine animals grow thickly and rapidly upon submerged objects. Even in depths of 100 feet or more, submerged objects quickly become covered with a thick growth of coral, a rock-like substance formed by thousands of tiny sea creatures that attach themselves to submerged objects and leave their shells behind when they die. One large wreck that had been lying on the bottom of the Red Sea for 300 years was covered with a layer of coral over a yard thick!

In order to recover such remains, it is necessary to smash through the coral with pneumatic drills—the kind that are used on land to drill holes in streets and sidewalks. Thus, in warm, shallow water, the chances that anything will be preserved are small indeed. Only in the best combination of circumstances—such as when the wreck is immediately covered by a layer of soft sand or mud—will sunken objects last more than a few years in such waters.

It sometimes happens that a large part of the cargo of a sunken ship becomes completely buried in the bottom of the sea, preserving everything in it. In one place on the coast of Israel, for example, a layer of

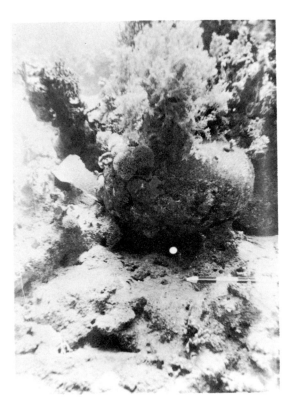

sand, pebbles, and seashells accumulated so rapidly that entire cargoes of ancient ships became completely buried soon after they sank. In some cases, not only the cargoes but also large sections of some very ancient ships have been dug out of the bottom of the sea.

A coral-covered jar found in the warm waters of the Red Sea

II TOOLS AND TECHNIQUES

The Archaeological Survey

Archaeologists who work under water face some special problems not encountered by their colleagues who work on land. The difference between making what is called an "archaeological survey" on land and in the water is a good illustration of this point. An archaeological survey is an exploration of a fairly large area made for the purpose of discovering where ancient objects may be found. When archaeologists make a survey of a piece of land or an area of the sea bottom, they must examine every square foot of the surface, looking for objects lying on top that might be clues to more objects buried underneath. They also draw detailed maps of the area, showing the location of all important natural features, such as trees, streams, marshes, caves, boulders, sand bars, and coral reefs.

On land, the archaeologist makes a survey on foot, walking slowly back and forth across the territory he is surveying. He can see an object 100 yards away, if it is not too small, and he can walk about two miles an hour, for five or six hours every day. At sea, however, things are not nearly so easy.

Suppose an archaeologist wants to survey a muddy sea bed that he hopes will contain some important remains of ancient shipwrecks. When he dives down to the bottom to look for clues on the surface of the bed, he will only be able to see one or two yards in any direction, because of the cloudiness of the water. If he is swimming against the current while peering with some difficulty through a diving mask into cloudy water, he will only be able to move along at about one-half mile per hour. If he went much faster than this, he might tire out too quickly or miss something important (or both). Because he is breathing air under high pressure, it is not safe for him to remain under the water for more than two hours a day.

A diver making an underwater survey

When the weather is bad, the seas become too rough for safety, and the archaeologists cannot dive at all. At other times, waves or ocean currents may cause the water to become muddier and cloudier than usual, and the diver would be able to see little. At such times, there may be no point in diving at all. Between bad weather and cloudy water conditions, the archaeologist can only work on the survey for about one out of every three days. When you put all these factors together, it can be calculated that if an archaeologist wanted to survey only one square mile of sea bottom by himself, it would take him about four *years* to do the job!

Obviously, some way had to be found for the underwater archaeologist to work faster and more efficiently. So in addition to the diving masks, compressed air tanks, special boats, air compressors, ropes, nets, and marking buoys that divers have been using for the last 20 years or so, some interesting new techniques and equipment have been recently developed to help the under-water archaeologist in his work.

Towing the Diver

One way of speeding up the process of making a survey is to free the diver from having to move along under his own power. A diver can be towed slowly by a boat, and this will enable him to concentrate all of his energies on the search for possible objects of interest on the sea bottom.

One of the simplest methods of towing consists of a wooden board connected by ropes to a boat. The board has two handles on it, which enable the diver both to hold on to the board and to steer it in any direction. Thus the diver can ride along near the surface, where he can see a large area of the sea bed, or he can dive down close to the bottom to inspect something that looks inter-esting.

While the diver is being towed along, maneuvering his board up and down in his inspection of the sea bed, the person who is navigating the boat will mark each area that has been inspected with floats or buoys to make sure that the entire area has been thoroughly covered. Every time the diver sees something that looks significant, he dives down for a closer look. Some of these things may just be rocks, sea animals, or patches of seaweed, and the diver will pass on. If they turn out to be something more interesting, how-ever, he will mark the spot so that he can return to it later on and investigate.

When making surveys of this type, the archaeologist will tow two to four divers at the same time. The divers are towed side by side, each with his own towing board. Working together in this way, several divers can cover a wider area and survey it more carefully than one diver could. A single diver might miss something because it passes beneath him while he is looking in a different direction, but not much of interest will escape the notice of three or four pairs of eyes!

Recently, a more advanced piece of equipment has been developed to replace the old wooden boards. This is a device called a "hydrodynamic cradle," and it looks something like an underwater sled. The hydro-dynamic cradle is basically an alu-minum platform partly covered by a transparent dome. The diver lies on the platform—just as you might lie down on a sled—and grasps two handles on either side of the cradle. By turning these handles, he can move the cradle up and down in the water, just as he could do with the wooden board.

But the hydrodynamic cradle has some things the old wooden board lacked. It has equipment that enables the diver to release a marking buoy over a certain spot just by pulling a lever. Some models even contain a communications system that keeps the diver in contact with the navigator of the boat.

Operating the hydrodynamic cradle requires skill and training. The cradle is designed for high-speed survey work, and it is towed at three miles per hour. (This is six times faster than a free-swimming diver can move.) The diver who is using the cradle must keep it properly balanced and steered as it moves through the water. At the same time, however, he must keep his eyes glued on the sea bottom. He must be able to recognize objects of archaeological interest almost instantly, so that he can release marker buoys whenever he spots something that will require close investigation.

There is yet another device for towing the diver, even larger and more complicated than the hydrodynamic cradle. This is a large, bell-shaped metal container called a "towvane." The towvane is large enough so that two divers can stand up inside it and look out at the sea bed through its plexiglass windows. There is even a telephone hookup to the towing boat! The towvane can be steered by means of flaps that the divers can move from the inside. Like the hydrodynamic cradle, the towvane is equipped with marking buoys that can be released from inside the apparatus itself.

The towvane is a complicated and expensive piece of equipment, and it is useful mainly when the water is clear enough so that the divers can see five or six yards in any direction. In some cases, the towvane is used to investigate a wreck that has already been located. Then it is simply dropped straight down into the water, like a diving bell. When it is used in this way, a section of the floor is cut out so that the divers can enter and leave the towvane at will.

The Cubmarine

No, that title is not misspelled. "Cubmarine" is the nickname that divers have given to the small,

The towvane

battery-powered submarines used for underwater research and exploration. These small ships are not designed to make voyages of their own at sea; instead they operate from a "mother" ship, which carries them out to the diving area. When the divers are ready to go, the cubmarine is lowered overboard and made ready for its descent to the sea bottom.

There are a number of different types of small research submarines in use and under development, and each is designed for slightly different needs and conditions. The simplest models can dive to a depth of about 200 feet, while the more advanced models are built to go far deeper. Some of them are steered by fins and rudders, while others are steered by jets of water that can be turned on momentarily to make corrections in the course of the underwater craft. These water jets operate on the same basic principle as the tiny rockets that are used to make course corrections in spacecraft.

The most sophisticated research submarines are equipped with mechanical arms and claws that can pick up and manipulate tools and sunken objects underneath the water. They also have powerful underwater lights and stereoscopic cameras, which can take three-dimensional pictures of the sea floor. With one such cubmarine, owned by the University of Pennsylvania, scientists discovered a sunken cargo along the coast of Turkey, in the eastern Mediterranean. Although this cargo was lying in the gloomy depths 125 feet below the surface, the small craft was able to conduct a thorough survey of this archaeological find and take a complete set of three-dimensional photographs of it in less than one hour!

The most advanced of these research submarines was recently designed by the American inventor Edwin Link. The ship carries a crew of four and is divided into two separate compartments. In one compartment, a scientist studies the sea floor and directs the progress of the survey, while a pilot actually navigates the craft. In the other compartment, two divers wait with their gear, ready to swim out of the ship and investigate anything interesting that might be discovered.

Substitutes For the Human Eye

It is sometimes difficult or impossible to send divers to the sea floor.

The water may be too cold, the currents may be too strong, or there may even be dangerous sea animals about. At other times, the divers themselves may be exhausted after several hours of work, or they may lack the necessary skill for some particularly difficult and dangerous job. For reasons such as these, scientists have developed techniques of surveying the sea bottom that use electronic equipment instead of the human eye. The first and most important of these techniques is called "sonar."

Sonar is to the sea what radar is to the skies—a method of detecting distant objects even in darkness or in cloudy conditions. Radar sends a beam of electronic signals (similar to radio waves) through the air; if the beam hits some object—like an airplane—it bounces back and shows up as a dot on a screen. Sonar sends a beam of sound waves through the water; this beam bounces off of solid objects and returns to the ship as an echo. It is then processed by electronic equipment, and it shows up as a line on a moving strip of paper.

Since the sonar beam is usually pointed down at the ocean floor, its most important job is to measure the depth of the bottom and to

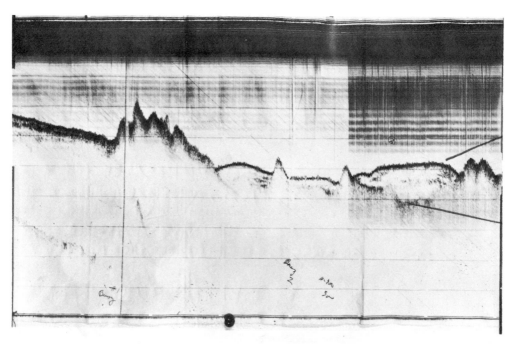

A graph produced by a sophisticated piece of sonar equipment known as a "boomer." The wavy line indicates the depth of the ocean and the shape of the ocean floor.

detect any large or unusual shapes that might be found there. Some of the newer types of sonar can not only record the shape of the ocean bottom but can even tell the difference between different types of ocean beds. Bottoms of hard rock, for example, will produce one type of signal, while soft mud or sand will produce another. An experienced sonar operator, working with the latest equipment, can tell a great deal about the bottom in a very short

time, as the ship cruises back and forth on the surface above.

Sonar has been used successfully not only to chart the shape and texture of the sea bottom but also to locate the wrecks of sunken ships. Sonar was first used in archaeological research in 1963, when it revealed the ruins of an ancient harbor in the eastern Mediterranean. It was next used to help locate the wreck of an English sailing ship that had escaped the Spanish Armada in the year

1588. Since then, sonar has been used to locate the remains of sunken ships and houses in the sea near Greece and in the Red Sea.

Until recently, there has been one large problem in using sonar. Because the beam of sound waves were fairly narrow, sonar could only be used to study the ocean bottom directly beneath the ship. Since the sonar could only "see" a narrow strip of sea floor as the ship cruised along, the survey ship had to sail back and forth a great many times in order to cover a sufficiently large area. If survey work was being done in the open sea, it was also necessary to use a very complex system of buoys and location markers to make sure that nothing was missed.

Now an improved type of sonar has been developed, called "side-scan sonar." This new type can send out and interpret a wide-angle beam, and a single ship can now survey a strip of ocean bottom more than a quarter of a mile wide! While the side-scan sonar is more complicated and much more difficult to operate, it has such an obvious advantage over the older type that it is sure to be used more and more often as time goes by.

Television can also serve as an electronic substitute for the human eye. If a survey is to be done some place where the water is clear, the archaeologist may decide to send a television camera down to inspect the sea floor instead of a human diver. Closed-circuit television equipment has been designed that can operate under water at considerable depths. Of course, a television camera does not tire out, experiences no health hazard by staying under water for many hours, and has little to fear from sharks or sting rays.

A typical television monitoring system has its own lights, which illuminate the sea floor in front of the camera. It is mounted on a device that enables it to be towed at a certain height above the bottom, pointing down at a controlled angle. Several cameras can be towed at the same time, and the scientists aboard ship can sit in the comfort of their sea-going laboratories and watch the ocean floor drift past on their television screens. If the archaeologist wishes, he can even make a tape recording of the underwater scene and play it back later, to watch again the underwater territory that the television camera had covered.

The main problem with underwater television is that it depends on the presence of two conditions that

Divers operating a metal detector

The last item in our list of electronic replacement for the human eye is a device called a "metal detector." Two different types of metal detectors are used by archaeologists. One is a simple, portable apparatus similar to the equipment used for detecting explosive mines. While this instrument is effective in identifying the presence of metal, it is not especially sensitive. It is necessary either for the metal object to be very large or for the detector to be very close to the object.

A much more sensitive type of metal detector, called a "proton magnetometer," has been developed by a British scientist. This device can detect even small metal objects at great distances. The proton magnetometer is large, heavy, and complicated, and it cannot be carried under the sea by a diver. Most of the apparatus is mounted on a ship, while the sensing device, called a "sensor," is towed some distance behind the ship.

In 1966, a proton magnetometer in the Mediterranean located iron objects weighing only a few pounds —at distances of more than 600 feet! This is much farther than any diver or underwater camera can see, even under the clearest conditions.

Developments in technology dur-

do not always exist in underwater work. First, the water must be clear, or else the camera will be unable to take a clear picture of the bottom. Second, the surface of the water must be calm. Otherwise, the motion of the ship bobbing up and down on the waves will cause the camera to bob up and down under the water. This would not only put a great strain on the wires and cables that connect the camera to the ship but also cause the television picture to bob up and down with the motion of the ship.

ing the past 20 years have made much useful equipment available to the underwater archaeologist, equipment that has greatly increased the speed and efficiency of the scientific work that must be done under the water. We have to remember, however, that these devices are merely tools that can only help – but not replace – the trained human diver.

The ancient objects that lie on the bottom of the sea are often so completely overgrown with sea life or submerged in the soft sand and mud that an untrained person could look right at them and never know they were there. Such remains would never be visible to a sonar device, because sonar only records the overall shape and texture of the sea floor. If the objects were made of wood, stone, fiber, or pottery—all of which were common materials in ancient times—they would, of course, be invisible to even the most sensitive metal detector. Television cameras would miss them too, because the television picture is not clear enough to show the fine details and the subtle differences in shape and texture that—to the trained eye— may signal the difference between a rock and an ancient pottery jug.

The trained human eye is, and always will be, the most important scientific instrument in underwater archaeology. There is a story about a small bay near the ruins of an old Crusader castle in Israel that illustrates this point. This small bay was filled with many interesting rock formations, and its waters swarmed with the fish and other sea creatures who made their homes among the nooks and crannies of these formations. The beauty and interest of this place was so great that it became a favorite spot for many skin divers. Over the years hundreds of divers explored the underwater formations and enjoyed the beautiful sea life.

Gradually, however, as some of the divers began to become experienced in underwater archaeology, they began to realize that the underwater formations they had been looking at all this time were, in fact, the ruins of an artificial harbor built many centuries earlier. As the harbor had fallen into ruin, the stone walls and piers gradually tumbled into the waters of the bay.

Just seeing something is not always enough. It is also necessary to understand the meaning of what you see. This is why the training and experience of the archaeologist is so important. Without it, no amount of fancy equipment will reveal the secrets of the ocean floor.

III THE MEDITERRANEAN SEA: BIRTHPLACE OF UNDERWATER ARCHAEOLOGY

The word "Mediterranean" means "center of the earth," and to the ancients this almost landlocked sea was indeed at the center of all things. On its northern shores were some of the great countries of Europe: Spain, France, Italy, and Greece. On its southern shores were the fertile North African lands of Morocco, Tunisia, and Egypt. On its eastern shores were the rich and civilized countries of Asia Minor, the Levant, and the Holy Land, and beyond these, the important trade routes to Arabia and to the fabulous civilizations of the East. To the west, the Mediterranean opened to the Atlantic Ocean through the Straits of Gibraltar. Just around the corner, and a short sail northward, were Portugal, the Netherlands, and England.

Since the Mediterranean has, in fact, been at the center of the civilized world from earliest times, it was only natural that ancient people began sailing across and around this important sea as soon as they built vessels large enough to carry them across the large distances from one safe harbor to another. Some of these sea voyages were for the purpose of trade, others for warfare, and still others for exploration colonization. Whatever the purpose of the voyages, however, the ancient ships usually carried money and provisions on board. When the ships encountered disaster and sank, treasures of ancient cargo fell to the bottom of the sea.

Right: A piece of pottery disguised by the beautiful coral that grows in the Red Sea

Overleaf left: These divers are operating an "air lift," a kind of vacuum cleaner used to excavate underwater ruins.

Overleaf right: Jars and pots from a shipwreck found in the Red Sea. The 300-year-old ship was carrying a cargo of mercury. (See the text on pp. 56–61.)

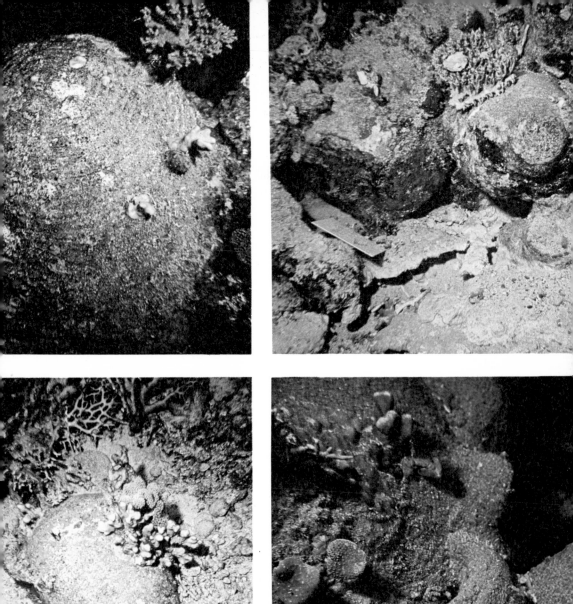

This is why the Mediterranean is so important in the study of underwater archaeology. Probably no other body of water has been more heavily traveled by as many different societies for so many years, and there is probably no other sea with as many sunken cargoes and wrecks waiting on the bottom for someone to discover them. We will describe some of the history of underwater archaeology in the Mediterranean a little later in this chapter. But first, there are some things you should know about the Mediterranean itself.

The Sea in the Middle of the Earth

Since very ancient times, the Mediterranean Sea has been a kind of highway that people of different societies have used to contact one another. The Pharaohs of Egypt sent their ships out to lands beyond the narrow Nile River Valley where their ancient civilization had flourished. The great imperial armies of Persia and Asia Minor sailed the Mediterranean as conquerors, subjugating many of the lands of the West. Later, the armies of ancient Greece and Rome traveled eastward, conquering the cities of Persia and Asia Minor and founding their own great empires.

Long after the fall of Greek and Roman civilization, the Crusaders of Europe set out in the ships of Italian merchants to drive the Moslems out of the Holy Land. When the Turks came to rule Asia Minor several hundred years later, however, the Turkish navies closed the eastern part of the Mediterranean to European ships. At the same time, pirates from the North African lands of Algeria and Morocco preyed on European merchant ships that strayed too far from the ports of Spain, France, and Italy. The Europeans' desire to continue their profitable trade with India and the Far East spurred them to seek new trade routes beyond the Mediterranean, a search that led to Columbus' voyage and the discovery of the New World.

In modern times, the Mediterranean Sea has continued to play a strategic role in world history. During the 19th century, the rich and powerful nations of Western Europe —especially Britain and France— struggled for control of the two strategic openings of this central sea: the natural one at the Straits of Gibraltar in the west and the man-made opening at the Suez Canal in the east. In the 20th century, the Mediterranean has continued to be strategically vital to the interests of the great world powers. It was the

Left: An amphora, or wine jar, encrusted with marine life

scene of many crucial struggles during World War II, as the Axis and the Allied powers fought for control of its sea routes. In recent years it has been the scene of the growing naval rivalry between the United States and Russia.

The Mediterranean is a rather tame body of water compared to the open oceans. It has only minor tides and a few strong currents. Unlike the strong trade winds of the open oceans, which come and go — and even change direction — with the changing seasons, the Mediterranean winds are usually gentle and do not vary tremendously from one time of year to another. Even during storms (which are rarely as violent as the hurricans and typhoons of the world's oceans), the waves of the Mediterranean reach barely half the height of those of the Atlantic. Even so, the storm-tossed Mediterranean seas sometimes reach heights of more than 25 feet. This is quite large enough to smash even the largest and strongest of the wooden vessels that ancient people possessed.

Over the centuries, the water level of the Mediterranean has changed from time to time. This is the main reason why buildings, harbors, and even entire villages have become submerged in the sea. People some-times build structures right at the edge of the water; if the water level rises, these structures may become submerged. A dock or pier, for example, is not of much use if it is located 50 feet from the water's edge, yet it may require only a small change in the level of the sea for a dock or pier to become either stranded on shore or submerged beneath the water.

There are two main reasons why water levels may change. One is that the amount of water in the oceans themselves may change. At some periods in our planet's history, the earth has been very warm, and most of the land has been covered with swamps and jungles. At other times, the earth has been much cooler, and great sheets of ice have slowly spread over the extreme northern and southern regions. The huge ice sheets that form during these cold periods contain a significant per-centage of the earth's water, and as they grow larger, the level of the seas and oceans drops. Just the opposite occurs during warm periods. As the great ice sheets melt, the seas fill with the water they release, and large areas of land become submerged.

Such enormous changes in the earth's temperature and the level of

This Roman harbor was once connected to the sea by the Tiber River, but gradual changes in the riverbed have left the harbor without an outlet. It is now over two miles away from the coast.

the oceans do not occur often, nor do they take place quickly. It has been a long time since the last ice age, longer ago than the entire history of human civilization. But although there have been only small changes in the earth's climate during the past few thousand years, these changes have been great enough to cause some variations in the level of the Mediterranean.

The other important reason for the change in sea level is that the land itself can rise or fall. Sometimes this happens suddenly and violently, accompanied by earthquakes and tidal waves. At other times, it happens very slowly and gradually, so that it is almost impossible to detect, except after the passage of many years. But it does not take a very rapid change in the height of the land to affect the water level at the shoreline. For example, if some spot at the water's edge had begun to sink at the rate of one inch per year when Columbus left on his voyage of discovery, that spot would now be under more than 40 feet of water.

The Birth of Underwater Archaeology

One day around the beginning of this century, some Greek fishermen were diving for sponges in the Greek islands. Suddenly one of the divers emerged from the depths, almost hysterical with excitement. "I have just seen a city under the sea!" he screamed. "It is filled with horses and people — even naked women!" The diver had seen the remains of an ancient shipwreck, one that had occurred before the time of Christ. The ship that had sunk had been carrying a cargo of statues made of marble and bronze.

Following this discovery, the Greek government conducted a salvage operation to bring as many of these priceless works of art to the surface as possible. One of these objects was a bronze statue of a youth that has since become famous. It is one of the finest ancient bronze statues ever discovered.

In the early days of underwater archaeology, the emphasis was on recovering objects from under the water. The idea was to quickly haul as much as possible to the surface, clean the objects that were found, and display them as curiosities in museums. As the science of archaeology developed, however, it became clear that much can be learned from a ruin or a shipwreck by carefully studying the remains *before* trying to take them out of the site where they are found.

Sometimes, for example, it is important to know which objects were lying on top of the pile and which were lying on the bottom, or which direction something was facing when it was found. This type of information may not always seem important at the time the remains are excavated, but it may later turn out to provide important clues about how and when a shipwreck occurred or an earthquake struck. If no record was made of these details when the wreck was first taken apart, then the information is lost forever.

The modern archaeologist is horrified by the idea of simply hauling objects to the surface as quickly and cheaply as possible. This would seem as wasteful and destructive as the thought of studying the workings of an alarm clock by first smashing it to bits with a hammer and then examining the pieces. The point is that the relationship of the objects to each other may be every bit as important as the size, shape, and characteristics of the individual objects themselves.

The first exploration of an underwater site using the new scientific methods occurred when a team of divers decided to excavate the remains of a Roman ship that lay on the bottom of the Mediterranean,

The bronze statue of a youth found in the ocean near Greece

near the French port of Marseilles. This team was headed by Jacques Cousteau, the pioneering diver, underwater explorer, naturalist, and conservationist, with his long-time collaborator Frederick Dumas. Cousteau and Dumas had earlier pioneered in developing the aqualung, and now they used underwater photography for the first time to create a photographic map of the site and to record the objects as they were removed from the wreck. They also invented a revolutionary new technique for raising sunken objects to the surface.

Previously, when divers wanted to bring objects to the surface, they used ropes and grappling hooks. This technique works perfectly well with hard, heavy objects like marble columns or cast-iron anchors. Such objects are not particularly fragile, and the pressure of the ropes around them does not damage them significantly. But when divers wanted to raise an entire ship to the surface, the hooks and ropes would be useless. An old wooden hull, half rotten from its years under the sea, would be crushed by the tightly encircling ropes or torn apart by the sharp grappling hooks.

In considering the problem of raising the old Roman ship, Cousteau and Dumas hit upon the idea of filling the hull itself with air. The gentle upward pressure of the air bubbles, pressing steadily and with equal force over a large area of the wreck, caused it to become buoyant, like a balloon, and to rise to the surface. The method worked so well that it has now become one of the underwater archaeologist's standard techniques.

The careful work done by Cousteau and Dumas was then greatly improved upon a few years later by another French underwater explorer, Philip Taillez. Working on the wreck of a ship called the *Titan*, discovered near the city of Marseilles, in France, Taillez made a careful record of the entire shipwreck just as it was found. As the excavation progressed, each stage of the excavation was photographed in detail. Taillez worked so carefully that, in addition to the many large objects that he recovered, even small things that had been aboard the ship when it went down, such as coins and even some almonds, were detected, recorded, and carefully preserved.

While the French team under Taillez was exploring the wreck of the *Titan*, an Italian team was excavating a Roman ship that had been discovered in about 50 feet of water near the island of Sardinia. These workers made still more advances in underwater archaeological techniques.

The Italian team made a map of the entire site and divided this map into many small squares. This collection of squares is called a "grid," and it is extremely useful in locating the exact position of some object

This large collection of amphoras was discovered in the wreck of a Roman ship excavated by Jacques Cousteau and Frederick Dumas.

on a map. You can find a common example of the use of a grid in mapping just by looking at an ordinary road map. The entire map will be divided into squares, so that when you are looking for a particular street or road, you will know what part of the map to look at. Archaeological grids are similar, except that the squares are usually smaller and more numerous, so that the various objects on the grid can be located with great exactness.

The other important advance in archaeological technique made by the Italian team has a long and impressive-sounding name: "photomosaic documentation." This term describes a method of making a large picture out of many small ones. First, the scientist takes a large number of photographs, making sure that he covers every section of the total area. Then he assembles the photographs into a mosaic (a picture made up of many small pieces fitted together to create a whole pattern or design). You may have seen examples of this technique in satellite photographs of large areas of land. It is often possible to see the lines where the different individual photographs were joined together to make the mosaic.

The Gelidonya Wreck

One of the most interesting and important events in the history of underwater archaeology occurred when a journalist and photographer named Peter Throckmorton decided to pursue his interest in archaeology and investigate some of the ancient shipwrecks along the coast of Greece and Turkey.

Throckmorton joined a team of Turkish sponge divers, and he lived and worked with them for a year. He shared their bread and their hardships, learned their language, listened to their stories, and gradually gained their confidence. Little by little, they revealed to him the great knowledge they had of the sea bottom. Throckmorton dove with his Turkish friends as they fished for sponges, and during these dives he discovered dozens of sites of shipwrecks that no one else knew about. During his time with the sponge fishermen, he carefully recorded the location of these sites, so that he and others could return to make more thorough investigations later on.

In 1960, Throckmorton returned to the United States and went to see Dr. George Bass, Professor of Classical Archaeology at the University of Pennsylvania. He told Dr. Bass

This diver is measuring a copper ingot found in the Cape Gelidonya wreck.

about his discoveries, and the archaeologist returned with him to the coast of Turkey to look at some of these ancient shipwrecks for himself. Excited and enthusiastic about what he saw, Dr. Bass organized a scientific team comprised of experts from a number of different countries. The team went to work on one of the most interesting of Throckmorton's discoveries: the Gelidonya wreck.

This shipwreck, located at Cape Gelidonya on the Turkish coast, consisted of a ship and its cargo that had been built and sailed by the ancient inhabitants of the Holy Land more than a thousand years before the birth of Christ. The ship has been carrying a cargo of copper and bronze pieces, tools made of these materials, and the equipment of a coppersmith's workshop. At

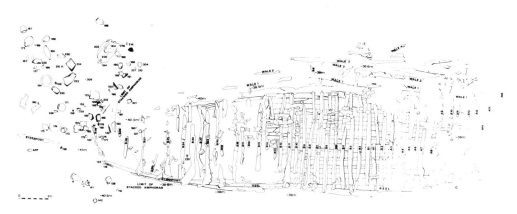

A diagram of the remains of a wrecked ship found near the island of Yassi Ada, off the coast of Turkey. (See the text on p. 48.)

that time, the Gelidonya wreck was the oldest shipwreck that had ever been discovered.

The team faced many difficult problems, including some dangerous ocean currents and the physical problems of deep diving (the wreck was nearly 100 feet below the surface). Yet the findings were precisely recorded, and heavily encrusted objects were removed from the sea bed with a minimum of damage. Objects of wood and metal —nearly destroyed by over 3,000 years in the sea—were successfully removed from the wreck, reconstructed and repaired, and preserved for future generations. In many respects, the work done at Cape Gelidonya was an important milestone in the history of underwater archaeology.

In addition to Peter Throckmorton and Dr. George Bass, the name of another pioneer of underwater archaeology is associated with the excavations of the Gelidonya wreck. It is Frederick Dumas, who had earlier collaborated with Jacques Cousteau in the original development of the aqualung. Dumas developed techniques for surveying and excavating underwater remains that became the basis for many of the methods still in use today.

Besides being a careful research worker, Dumas was also a superb diver who could work quickly, carefully, and effectively under water. Until that time, many scientists doubted that it was possible to conduct careful scientific research in the cold, dark, dangerous depths of the sea bottom. But Dumas proved once and for all that underwater archaeology was not simply an optimistic dream. His work paved the way for the new breed of scientists who have followed his achievements.

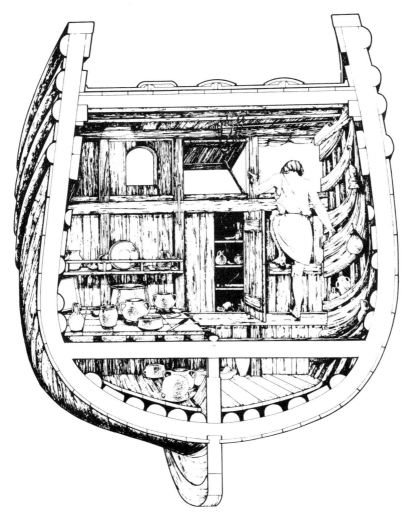

An artist's reconstruction of the stern of the Yassi Ada ship

IV SHIPWRECKS AND SCIENCE

Numerous wrecks of ancient ships have been discovered and explored since the pioneering work of the first underwater archaeologists. Some of these excavations yielded entirely new kinds of information, and all of them have added to our knowledge about shipbuilding and seafaring in past times. Archaeologists have studied far too many shipwrecks to be described in this small book, but we thought you might like to know about some of the most interesting and important of these underwater explorations.

The Wreck of Yassi Ada

Near the island of Yassi Ada, off the Turkish coast, scientists found the remains of a Byzantine merchant ship dating from the seventh century A.D. (The Byzantines ruled the area around Greece, Asia Minor, and the Holy Land after the fall of Rome.) Every splinter of wood was collected and carefully reassembled, until the archaeologists could describe in detail not only the exact size and shape of the boat but even the methods that the ancient Byzantines had used in its construction.

This careful scientific work also produced a wealth of information about the loading capacity, means of propulsion, and type of anchors used at this period in history. Archaeologists even got a glimpse of the personal lives of ordinary Byzantine sailors when they found a number of utensils and other personal belongings in the wreck. Finally, this particular exploration greatly expanded our knowledge about how water-logged wood survives over the centuries and how it can be recovered and preserved.

A Cargo of Coffins

In the 1960s, Peter Throckmorton excavated the wreck of a ship near the Italian coast that dated from the time of the Roman Empire. Throckmorton's research yielded much valuable and detailed information about shipbuilding in Roman times. It showed how the Roman shipbuilders used various types of wood, such as pine, cypress, and cedar. The research also yielded information about the shapes of the nails used in ship construction. Finally, Throckmorton showed how the bottoms of the ships were covered with large sheets of lead. This was done to protect the hull of the ship from damage by marine animals.

But perhaps the strangest and most interesting aspect of this wreck was the nature of its cargo. When the ship went down, it was carrying a load of coffins, obviously meant for the rich and important citizens of the Empire. The coffins had been carved out of marble, and they had been brought by sea all the way from Asia Minor in the east. We may sometimes think of these ancient ships as puny little wooden craft, and it is true that in comparison with

The cargo of marble coffins found by Peter Throckmorton

our giant tankers, aircraft carriers, and ocean liners, the old wooden ships were small indeed. Still, they were not exactly rowboats. The marble coffins aboard this single wooden ship weighed more than 150 tons!

This was not the only time that such heavy cargoes were found in ancient shipwrecks. A Roman ship found near the town of San Pietro in southern Italy also carried a cargo of marble coffins. Another shipwreck dating from a time after the fall of Rome had a cargo of precut pieces of marble intended to be used in building a church.

The Greek Amphoras of Kyrenia

The complex and sophisticated electronic equipment now used for underwater survey work has produced some valuable finds, but the knowledge possessed by local divers and fishermen is still sometimes the most valuable aid to archaeologists. One example of this is the experience of a team of American archaeologists, headed by Professor M. Katzev, that undertook a survey of the waters around the island of Cyprus, looking for ancient shipwrecks. (Cyprus is a large island off the southern coast of Turkey; it was an important center of Greek trade and commerce in ancient times.) After nearly a month of careful surveying that yielded virtually nothing, the team was discouraged and about to abandon its search.

Then a local fisherman took the scientists to a spot about two miles offshore, near the harbor of Kyrenia on the north coast of the island. Some time ago, the fisherman had seen a heap of ancient pottery wine jars called "amphoras," lying on the sandy sea bottom in about 100 feet of water. As it turned out, the wine-flasks were just the tip of the iceberg: underneath them was a mound of cargo and the ruins of an ancient Greek merchant ship dating from the fourth century B.C.!

Professor Katzev returned to Kyrenia with a team of more than 40 scientists, students, and professional divers. During the warm months of 1968 and 1969, this army of investigators spent thousands of hours on the sea bottom. They found more than 400 amphoras and several millstones for grinding grain. The ruins were in such excellent condition that even the shells of the almonds that were part of the ship's cargo were perfectly preserved.

One of the most impressive accomplishments of this expedition was the successful raising of most of

he hull of the Kyrenia wreck. Part of the ship's cargo of amphoras can be seen on the right. The heavy
illstones in the center of the picture were probably used as ballast..

the ship's hull to the surface. This was an extremely difficult task for a ship of this age, because the wood was so completely rotten that it had no strength of its own. So the divers cut the entire ship into small sections, marked and labelled each section for future reassembly, and packed the sections into special containers. Only then were the ship's remains raised to the surface.

Afterwards, each scrap of wood was given a long and complicated treatment of drying and preservation. This ship is now being reconstructed, and it will be put on display at the Kyrenia Castle when its reconstruction is finished, complete with its ancient cargo of wine-flasks and other goods.

The Figurines of Shave-Ziyyon

One of the most important archaeological sites ever found in the Mediterranean was first discovered by an Israeli fisherman. In the sea near the village of Shave-Ziyyon, the fisherman came across a number of curious tube-shaped objects thickly encrusted with sea life. He brought these strange objects to the Haifa University in northern Israel. When the museum workers cleaned off the encrustation, they discovered that the objects were actually pottery figurines. The figurines had been made by the ancient Phoenicians, a trading and seafaring people who lived on the coast of the eastern Mediterranean — in what is now the territory of Israel and Lebanon — before the time of the ancient Greeks.

Even more interesting was the fact that some of the figurines bore the marks of the "sign of Tanit." Tanit — the Phoenician goddess of love and fertility — was the patron goddess of the North African city of Carthage. Carthage had begun its history as a Phoenician colony, established around the eighth century B.C., and it had grown into a wealthy and powerful outpost of eastern civilization in the western Mediterranean.

The Carthaginians maintained close ties with their Phoenician homeland and carried on a vigorous trade with the other Phoenician cities, bringing them slaves, grain, metals, and precious stones in exchange for cloth and other luxury items. Clearly, the figurines had been part of a Carthaginian cargo, bound for one of the Phoenician ports. Shave-Ziyyon itself, in fact, is just north of the Israeli city of Acco, the site of the ancient Phoenician port of Acre.

Pottery figurines of the Phoenician goddess Tanit, found in the sea near Shave-Ziyyon

After examining the pottery figurines, the Haifa University organized an expedition to investigate this site. Their divers and archaeologists found a cargo of heavily encrusted amphoras and other objects scattered over a large area of the sea floor. But the most important aspect of this find was the discovery of more figurines—literally hundreds of them—forming one of the largest collections of pottery figurines ever found at a single location. Archaeologists and historians are now studying this wealth of material. From it they hope to learn much about the relationship between the Phoenician homeland and the far-flung Phoenician colonies during the years around 500 B.C. This was the time when the civilization of ancient Greece began to dominate the Mediterranean, overshadowing the Phoenicians, who had been the first great sea power of the ancient world and from whom the Greeks had learned much of what they knew.

A Carthaginian Warship

You may have noticed that all the shipwrecks we have described so far have been merchant vessels. Yet there were numerous warships in ancient times, a fact we know from historical records. Many great sea battles were fought on the Mediterranean over the centuries, and some of them involved hundreds of fighting ships. Many warships were sunk in these battles, yet very few sunken warships have ever been found on the sea bottom.

There are two main reasons why the sunken warships have almost completely disappeared. The first reason has to do with size: warships were generally rather small vessels. This is because ancient seafarers depended more upon oarsmen than on sails to provide their motive power. A large boat is difficult to row, and it tends to move along very slowly, while a smaller and narrower boat can move along with surprising speed under oar power. The warships of ancient times had to be fast, and, in order to be fast, they had to be small. Small boats are less likely to survive for long periods on the sea bottom than large boats, because they are more likely to be tossed about by waves and currents. Thus they are more easily broken apart.

The second reason for the rapid destruction of warships is that they carried no cargo. When a wooden ship goes down under the weight of 150 tons of stone coffins, you can be sure that it will stay right where it lands on the sea bottom. Cargoes of metal, pottery, and building materials are almost as effective in keeping the sunken ship in place. These cargoes not only pin down the wreck, but they also bury parts of it and thus preserve these parts from the destructive action of the waves, currents, and sea life. For this reason, merchant ships and their cargo tend to survive, while the empty hulls of warships, resting lightly on the sea floor, are quickly destroyed.

You may recall, however, that mud and sand are excellent preservative materials under water. This is exactly why a warship built by the ancient seafaring Phoenicians turned up recently in excellent condition.

At about the same time that the Haifa University was investigating the discovery of the strange Phoenician figurines, the wreck of a Carthaginian warship was found in water only 10 feet deep, off the island of Motya, near Sicily. The entire ship had been covered by a thick layer of sand, and thus it had been fairly well preserved, even though it was in shallow water.

The wreck of this warship is now being excavated by Honor Frost, an archaeologist who began her career many years ago, working with Jacques Cousteau, Frederick Dumas, Dr. George Bass, and Peter Throckmorton on the old Gelidonya wreck expedition. She has so far retrieved planking, frames, floor timbers, and other parts of the ship. This ship has, in fact, been preserved so well that in some places it is still possible to see the lines and markings made by the ancient carpenters as they measured and cut the various pieces of the ship for construction.

Shipwrecks in the Red Sea

For nearly 1,000 miles of their coastlines, the great land masses of Africa and Asia are separated by only about 150 miles of water. The body of water that lies between them is called the "Red Sea." It is about half the length of the Mediterranean Sea and shaped somewhat like a jagged knife blade. At its southern end, the Red Sea narrows to a width of 20 miles before it opens into the Indian Ocean, while in the north it reaches nearly to the Mediterranean before ending altogether.

In ancient times, it took only a short overland journey through Egypt to get from the Red Sea to the shores of the Mediterranean; in modern times, the Suez Canal allows

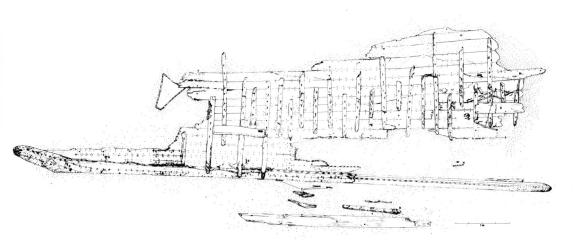

A plan of the wreck of a Carthaginian warship discovered near Motya. The excavation of this wreck has just begun, but from it archaeologists may eventually learn much about the construction of ancient warships.

ocean-going vessels to pass from one body of water to the other. Throughout most of recorded history, the Red Sea has been a waterway of tremendous importance in trade and commerce. The ancient Egyptians and Hebrews, for example, used the Red Sea to bring ores and precious metals from distant mines to their great capital cities.

In some ways, the Red Sea might seem to be an ideal place to look for ancient shipwrecks, since the coastline is often rocky and dangerous and the waters are unusually clear. But archaeologists have searched in vain for the remains of the ancient boats that are known—from historical accounts—to have sailed (and occasionally sunk) in these waters. There is simply nothing to be seen.

The answer to this riddle lies in the nature of the Red Sea itself: its warm waters are an excellent environment for the growth of coral. In fact, coral grows so quickly in the Red Sea that anything which falls to the bottom is quickly encrusted with a thick layer of the tiny animals. They deposit their rock-like shell material, generation after generation, layer after layer, until the object is hidden from view.

King Solomon's ships sailed the Red Sea waters, and no doubt some of these vessels were lost in storms and are lying on the bottom, waiting for an archaeologist to uncover them. The ships of King Solomon would make a fascinating and exciting discovery, but the problem of the coral must be solved before these ships can ever be found. Scientists have calculated that anything which fell to the bottom of the Red Sea in King Solomon's day would now be under a layer of coral 25 to 30 feet thick, roughly the height of a two-story building!

One of the few shipwrecks that have been discovered in the Red Sea is the remains of a Turkish ship about 250 years old. Fortunately for the archaeologists, the ship went down in a shallow bay where currents of muddy water emptying into the Red Sea helped to retard the growth of coral. Not a trace of

the upper part of the ship could be found, and archaeologists believe that it must have caught fire and burned to ashes above the waterline.

The ship's cargo was, however, more or less intact. It consisted of a huge amount of pottery, including more than 1,000 amphoras, a number of clay pipes, and some pieces of Chinese porcelain. The style of the pottery and the way in which it is decorated suggest that it is Turkish and Arabian. Nevertheless, no pottery quite like this has ever been found, and its exact origin is still something of a mystery to the experts.

One of the most interesting archaeological finds from the Red Sea was discovered by an underwater photographer only about five miles from the shallow bay where the wreck of the Turkish ship was found. When the photographer was returning to the surface after a dive, he noticed, almost hidden in the dense growth of coral, a number of huge round jars and several bowls made of bronze. Upon his return, he notified the Israeli archaeological authorities and sent them some photographs he had taken of the site.

The archaeologists located the huge jars and bronze utensils in the middle of a beautiful formation of

Writing on a sheet of plastic, a diver makes a detailed record of the remains of a wrecked ship. Each piece of wood in the wreck has been marked with a plastic tag for purposes of identification.

A collection of unusual pottery jars was found in this 250-year-old shipwreck in the Red Sea.

coral, and they decided to remove the ancient objects from the coral reefs in such a way as to damage the coral as little as possible. When the jars and bowls had been recovered and could be examined more closely, the scientists noticed some small droplets of a bright silvery color on the inside of some of these containers. They turned out to be droplets of mercury—the liquid metal used in thermometers — which evidently comprised part of the ship's cargo. The mercury was probably being used in the process of smelting and purifying gold.

It is interesting to note that the bronze bowls found in the ship-

An archaeologist draws a picture of underwater finds, using a section of a metal grid as a framework for his drawings. Such grids help underwater archaeologists to keep accurate records of their discoveries

wreck are not made out of ordinary bronze but of bronze that contains more than 20 percent lead. Ordinary bronze—which is basically a mixture of copper and tin—often contains no lead at all. The presence of lead makes bronze resistant to corrosion by mercury. This finding established beyond doubt that the bronze bowls and utensils were also used in the chemical processes for which the mercury was intended.

This particular wreck was about 300 years old; thus both of the shipwrecks found so far in the Red Sea are of comparatively recent origin.

Two large jars from the wrecked ship that carried mercury in its cargo

This Viking ship was discovered in a waterway leading to Roskilde, the ancient capital of Denmark.

Archaeologists believe that there may be dozens or even hundreds of other wrecks, stretching back thousands of years in time, lying undiscovered under the thick coral blanket of the Red Sea bottom.

Someday, science may find ways of locating these wrecks, and the archaeologists may find ways of digging them out of the coral reefs without destroying the natural beauty of the underwater environment. Until then, the corals of the Red Sea will keep their secrets well guarded.

Shipwrecks in the English Mud

In the year 1910, construction workers in London were digging the foundation of a new public building that was to be erected near Westminster Bridge. As they were removing the damp earth, they suddenly came upon the remains of a wooden ship. Experts on ancient history were called to the scene, and they identified the ship as a Roman merchant vessel.

Later, an amateur British archaeologist, exploring the banks of an English riverbed, discovered the remains of three boats of primitive design. They turned out to be extremely ancient — scientists estimate that they were built in the Roman period. These boats, constructed of wooden strips lashed together, are the only examples of this type known to science.

In 1962, construction workers digging a foundation on the banks of the Thames River in London struck some large oak planks deep in the earth. Archaeologists were called in, and they built a dividing barrier to seal off the site from the waters of the river nearby. The mud and shallow water were pumped out, and the ancient remains were carefully removed. They proved to be the wrecks of two river boats built during the second century A.D.

In all these cases, ships that had sunk and become stuck in the mud of a river bottom or riverbank were covered — and thus protected from decay — by a thick layer of mud deposited by the river itself. In our final example, however, an entire ship seems to have been deliberately buried by the people who used it.

In 1939, British archaeologists were excavating a burial mound used by the ancient Saxons, inhabitants of northern Germany who came to settle in England after the fall of Rome. Quite unexpectedly, their shovels struck the remains of a large hull built in the style of the sea-going boats used by the Vikings.

The ship was unearthed and re-constructed, following the methods used by Norwegian archaeologists, who had already unearthed and reconstructed Viking ships found in Norwegian burial mounds.

The Great European Sailing Ships

Many other ships that have been found and explored by archaeologists do not date from ancient times. It would take far more space than we have to describe them, but we should mention some of them before moving on to the next chapter.

One of these more recent ship-wrecks is that of the *Vasa*, built to be the flagship of the Swedish navy in 1628 and sunk within an hour after it was launched in Stockholm Bay. The raising and restoring of this ship by the Swedish government in 1960 was the most thorough, well-organized, and expensive project in the history of underwater archaeology. The *Vasa* is now housed in a building constructed especially for it, and it has become one of Europe's most unusual archaeological museums.

On the other side of the Atlantic, underwater archaeologists have spent many years of work trying to locate and study the shipwrecks of the Spanish "gold fleet." After the conquest of the Americas, these transoceanic sailing vessels crossed the Atlantic between Spain and the New World for two centuries. They often carried treasures in gold in addition to their cargoes of food, livestock, and manufactured goods. But between the pirates who abounded in Caribbean waters and the sudden and violent storms of the area, many Spanish ships were lost, treasure and all.

The archaeologists who have spent their careers searching for and exploring these wrecks have had one of the most difficult jobs of all underwater scientists. They have not only had to cope with the problems and dangers of the sea, but they have also had to deal with the treasure hunters and occasional thieves who are searching for the same wrecks. After all, some of the treasures in gold that divers have found in the Caribbean have been worth hundreds of thousands of dollars. With such riches at stake, the search for old shipwrecks becomes more than a battle against the elements.

But the scientist has at least one advantage over the treasure hunter. The weeks or months spent diving and exploring a shipwreck may be a waste of time if your only interest is the gold that the wreck may contain.

The *Vasa* is towed to land after being raised from the bottom of Stockholm Bay. The metal structure surrounding the ship became the framework for the building constructed to house it.

But the archaeologist's most important reward is knowledge, and thus his time is rarely ever wasted. With each dive, he learns something about the past that no one knew before. The excitement and fulfillment of this continual discovery is the archaeologist's true gold.

V   RUINED HARBORS AND SUNKEN CITIES

In the days before the development of cities and seaports, people anchored and unloaded their boats in river mouths and bays. Such natural harbors were sufficient to shelter the small, open boats that people used in those days. In fact, many of these boats were small enough to be dragged out of the water completely if the weather got too rough.

But when people started building cities and engaging in commerce with distant lands, they also began to build larger and larger boats. Ancient writings describe ships used more than 1,000 years before the birth of Christ that were triple the size of the ships Columbus used when he sailed to the New World! These huge ships needed special facilities that natural harbors could not provide. They required protection from the waves of the open sea, sufficiently deep water to approach the shore without fear of scraping the bottom, and a place to anchor or tie up, preferably where goods could be unloaded directly onto dry land.

The earliest type of harbor consisted of a sea wall that provided protection from the storm-tossed waves of the open sea and a place where the water was deep enough for large ships to anchor. Some of these early harbors also had storehouses on shore, where goods unloaded from the ships could be kept safe and dry.

Later, as maritime trade became more developed, the port cities of ancient seafaring nations began to build boat basins. A boat basin is like a huge swimming pool, with an entrance leading to it from the open sea. The sides of the boat basin are often nearly vertical, so that a boat can tie up alongside the edge of the land. The land around the boat basin is usually flat—and often paved—so that goods can be loaded onto or off the ship while it is tied to the dock.

The Phoenicians built boat basins

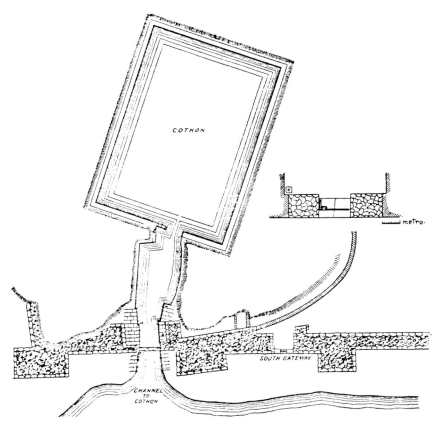

A drawing of the boat basin, or *cothon,* on the island of Motya. Ships entered the basin through the narrow channel shown at the bottom of the drawing.

for their great trading fleets, and one of these basins has survived on the island of Motya, near Sicily. (It was just outside Motya's boat basin that Honor Frost found the remains of a Phoenician warship.) The basin was about the size of a very large swimming pool, and the water in it was more than six feet deep. An artificial channel connected the boat basin with the open sea.

But Motya was only a small settlement. In some of the largest Phoenician cities, boat basins were much more complex, designed not only to harbor the Phoenician merchant ships but also to provide space for the Phoenician warships that often accompanied the merchantmen to protect them. The complex harbor at Carthage, for instance, consisted of three parts. The outermost part of the harbor was a long wall, called a "breakwater," which was built parallel to the coastline. By sailing into the narrow space between the breakwater and the shore, ships were safe from the violence of the sea. The waves would break against the side of the wall that faced the open sea, while the water on the other side of the wall would be calm. This breakwater was also designed to be used as a pier, and cargo could be loaded onto its wide surface.

Ships of foreign nations were allowed to use the breakwater, but only the ships of Carthage itself were allowed to enter the protected waters of the basin. The basin was roughly oval in shape, and the Carthaginian merchant fleet was anchored here. From this outer basin, a short channel led into a smaller inner basin shaped something like a doughnut. In the center of this ring-shaped body of water stood a building that housed the military command of the Carthaginian navy. It was here, in the innermost and most easily defended part of the harbor, that the Carthaginian warships were kept.

Such inner and outer harbors were typical of major Phoenician port cities. Two of the best examples are found in the Phoenician homeland, in the port cities of Tyre and Sidon. These great ancient seaports, located on the eastern coast of the Mediterranean, were the most famous of all Phoenician cities.

In the 1930s, two underwater archaeologists conducted pioneering investigations of the ruins of the harbor installations at Tyre and Sidon. They photographed the areas from the air, and the pictures revealed the vague outlines of the

Right: Marking a wreck site in the Red Sea

Overleaf left above: Divers at work. The diver on the left is removing coral encrustations from a large jar. On the right, divers examine a jar containing a drop of mercury.

Overleaf left below: Unusual bottle-shaped jars found in a shipwreck in the Red Sea

Overleaf right: A diver measures large "Ali-Baba" vessels from a Red Sea shipwreck.

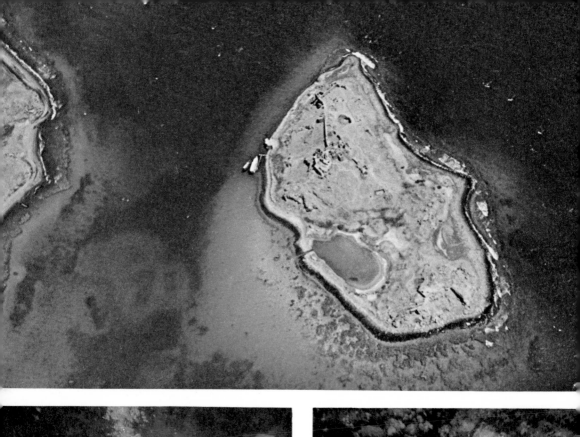

These workers are uncovering the remains of an ancient Phoenician harbor on the coast of present-day Syria.

underwater remains. Then they used divers to go beneath the surface and examine the old stones and walls in more detail. These harbors not only had breakwaters, deep anchorages,

Left above: This coral island in the Red Sea may be the site of an ancient harbor built by King Solomon.
Left below: The diver on the left is making a sketch of an ancient jar. The diver on the right is using an air lift to dig underwater finds out of a coral reef.

and inner and outer basins, but they also had piers as well. (Piers are platforms built out into the water; ships can be tied to them, and they also serve as convenient areas for loading cargo.) Thus these ancient harbors contained all the basic docking facilities offered by the most modern harbors in use today.

The Harbors of Ancient Greece
The Phoenicians were the first

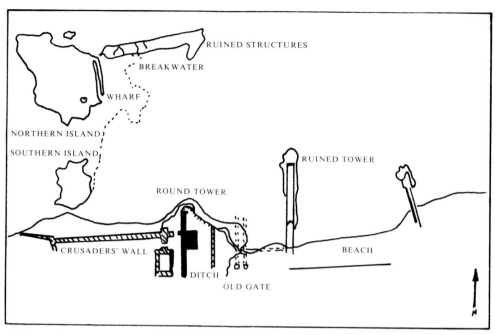

RUINED STRUCTURES

BREAKWATER

WHARF

NORTHERN ISLAND

SOUTHERN ISLAND

RUINED TOWER

ROUND TOWER

CRUSADERS' WALL

BEACH

DITCH

OLD GATE

N

A plan of the Phoenician port of Atlit

great seafaring people of the ancient world, but the Greeks eventually overshadowed them, becoming the greatest sea power the Mediterranean had ever seen. When the Greeks were beginning to expand their seafaring activities, the power and wealth of the Phoenicians had already begun to decline. The old Phoenician cities were vulnerable to attack by land, and the powerful Assyrian Empire to the east demanded tribute from them. The important Phoenician port of Sidon rebelled against the Assyrians and was destroyed in 677 B.C. The port of Tyre was permanently weakened by continual conflict with the Assyrians.

While the Phoenician decline continued, the Greeks were becoming more and more proficient at seafaring, and they began to need well-fortified and complex harbors to protect their growing fleet. The Greeks soon realized that it was important to maintain a fleet of warships to protect their merchant vessels and to fortify their harbors

This photograph of Atlit shows the port's ancient wharf (foreground) and the breakwater that sheltered it from the open sea.

so that they could be defended against raids from the sea.

One of the first things the Greeks did, therefore, was to build sea walls across the mouths of their harbors, leaving only narrow openings for the ships to pass through. At first, the Greeks knew almost nothing about constructing such things. The people of the island of Delos, for example, simply piled up large blocks of stone to make their crude but massive sea wall. Soon, however, the Greeks learned to build sea walls and piers more skillfully. They learned many of these new skills from the Phoenicians, whose improvements in harbor construction the Greeks copied to use in their own constantly improving maritime facilities.

When British divers explored a Greek harbor on the North African coast not many years ago, they discovered that the harbor had been constructed in several stages, roughly corresponding to this history of constantly improving knowledge and technique. First, a rough sea wall was built to shelter the harbor from the open sea. Then the area inside the harbor was enlarged. Next, a solid structure was built out into the water, containing piers and even shipyards (areas constructed espe-

cially for building and repairing ships). Finally, the harbor was divided into inner and outer sections to make it easier to defend.

Another harbor, this one on the Greek mainland, was constructed according to this same general plan. Because of changes in the water level in that location, the storerooms and houses of the ancient harbor settlement had become submerged in several feet of water. To make things worse, huge amounts of debris had washed up onto the ruin over the years. An archaeological team nevertheless succeeded in uncovering the ancient remains, despite the great problems that they had to overcome. The scientists not only acquired detailed information about an ancient harbor town, including the location of the various buildings, but they also recovered some articles of ancient furniture and unearthed the floors of many buildings, which were decorated with mosaics of colored glass.

King Herod's Great Achievement

In the years immediately before the birth of Christ, the Jewish king Herod the Great pursued a policy of building up the commercial strength of ancient Palestine, so as to rival the economic power of some of its

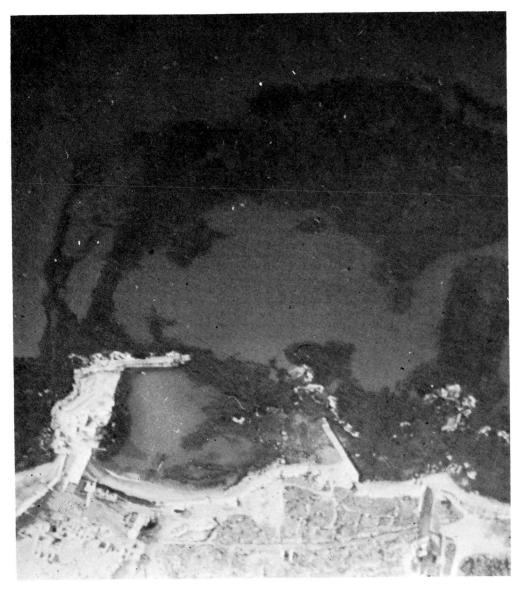

An aerial photograph of the great port of Caesarea, built by King Herod

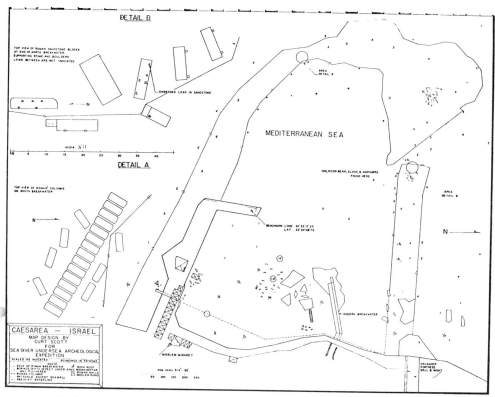

An archaeologist's map of Caesarea

neighbors. In order to carry out his plans, Herod needed a major seaport on the Mediterranean. Thus he built one of the greatest ports of ancient times along a stretch of the coast just south of the important Phoenician port cities. King Herod named this new port "Caesarea."

The ancient historian Josephus wrote about Herod's efforts, and he described how Caesarea's harbor had been constructed. According to Josephus, the king had begun construction by lowering gigantic blocks of stone into water 120 feet deep, to build a foundation for the structures that were to be erected at the harbors' outer edge. Each of these stone blocks was 50 feet long, 10 feet wide, and 9 feet high—roughly the size of a Greyhound bus! When the foundation had reached the surface of the water, the king built a pier on top of it that was 200 feet wide and approximately half a mile long. The seaward half of the pier served as a breakwater to protect the harbor from the waves, while the other half supported a massive stone wall that curved around to enclose the harbor. Massive towers were spaced along this wall, Josephus reported, and a row of arched shelters were erected to serve as resting places for the crews of newly arrived ships. On either side of the harbor's mouth there were three colossal statues standing on tall stone pillars.

While Josephus' descriptions painted a magnificent picture, archaeologists and historians were skeptical. How could such massive undertakings have been carried out with the primitive technology of ancient times? Most experts simply assumed that Josephus had been exaggerating. Certainly there was little visible evidence of the magnificent harbor he had described.

What had happened was that, over the centuries, earthquakes had gradually tumbled Caesarea's great harborworks into the sea, and the winds and waves had completed the process of destruction. But when an American expedition of archaeologists led by the inventor Edwin Link decided to survey the sunken remains of Caesarea in 1960, they were astounded to find that the harbor was really as huge as Josephus had described it to be. Even the giant blocks of stone were precisely the dimensions that Josephus has indicated. As a result of this discovery, the experts have gained new respect both for the accuracy of Josephus' descriptions and for the fantastic energy and engineering skill of King Herod's ancient builders.

A Story of Heroism

One of the most exciting and heroic chapters in the history of underwater archaeology occurred when Israeli divers and archaeologists fought to excavate the sea wall of the ancient Phoenician port of Acre. The modern city of Acco, built on the site of ancient Acre, did not have a sheltered harbor before 1965. In that year the authorities decided to protect the harbor from winter storms by building a breakwater, using the remains of the ancient Phoenician sea wall for a foundation. Israeli archaeologists were alarmed, since this new con-

An aerial photograph of the harbor at Acco. The ruins of the ancient sea wall can be seen extending upward from the point of land near the bottom of the picture.

struction would bury the remains of the original harbor permanently and make any further excavations at Acre impossible.

The archaeologists first tried to convince the authorities to delay the harbor project, or at least to provide money for a full-scale emergency expedition to excavate the remains before it was too late. But all their requests were denied. The government proceeded with its plans to begin construction on the new sea wall, giving the archaeologists nothing more than official permission to carry out whatever underwater research they wanted to do on their own. Thus, in the months of October and November of 1965, one of the strangest archaeological investigations of all times took place.

While divers worked frantically on the sea bed, the operators of heavy machinery went into action. There were times when archaeologists on the surface pleaded with the construction workers to wait even just a few hours before covering some spot with blocks of stone. There were other times when the crane operator would begin to lower the huge stone blocks into place before the divers had even come to the surface!

Meanwhile, the sailors and fishermen of Acco were growing angry. With winter fast approaching, they feared for the safety of their boats; they wanted the sea wall completed before the beginning of the winter storms. It was rumored that the project might not be finished for years if the archaeologists caused it to be delayed past the beginning of the first winter storms. Finally, the angry fishermen attacked the archaeologists' headquarters, took all the equipment they could get their hands on, and threw it into the sea.

Yet in spite of these overwhelming dangers and difficulties, the courageous and dedicated archaeologists collected the essential information about the ancient sea wall before it was too late. They not only succeeded in mapping the sea wall, but they were even able to determine the details of its construction. The archaeologists dug trenches under the sea bottom, discovering the foundations of a still older structure. In this structure, they found a piece of broken pottery with letters of the ancient Phoenician alphabet inscribed on it. There is still much work to be done at Acco, and many other parts of the harbor still remain to be investigated. But the ancient sea wall has provided archaeologists with valuable information that could have been lost forever.

Left, above, and below: The versatile air lift being used in underwater excavations

Archaeologist Robert Marx (right) displays some of the thousands of artifacts found in the ruins of Port Royal, Jamaica.

Port Royal, Jamaica

Located on the southern coast of the island of Jamaica, Port Royal was once one of the most prosperous seaports of the Caribbean. Throughout the 1600s, Port Royal was the colorful and crowded home of merchants, missionaries, smugglers, pirates, and drifters. It earned a reputation as one of the most wicked and wide-open cities of the New World. Some people even compared Port Royal to the biblical city of Sodom, which was destroyed by fire and earthquake thousands of years ago — in punishment, the Bible said, for its unrepentant wickedness.

In 1692, disaster struck Port Royal. A terrible earthquake destroyed almost the entire city, and its ruins sunk to 65 feet below the level of the sea. In the years that followed, the ruins of Port Royal — which could be dimly seen through the water from above — became the subject of tales of mystery and treasure. Finally, after World War II, a preliminary expedition made a survey and exploration of the sunken ruins. The members of the expedition concluded that the underwater remains could be excavated.

Several years passed, during which a full-scale expedition was organized under the direction of the American diver, treasure-hunter, and underwater archaeologist Robert Marx. Marx worked on the site of Port Royal for almost three years, under the most difficult and dangerous conditions. The sea itself was often cloudy and was infested with dangerous sharks, sting rays, and moray eels, yet Marx succeeded in excavating large sections of the city. He brought up thousands of artifacts, including objects of daily life such as household utensils, coins, tools, pipes, weapons, and pieces of fine pewter ware. Marx's work was, in fact, so thorough that he was even able to reconstruct the floor plans of several complete houses down to the tiniest details, including the exact location of each object found in the sunken house.

A Village in the Lake

In 1965, an Italian engineer was surveying the shore of a lake about 100 miles north of Rome, when he discovered what appeared to be archaeological remains. Peter Throckmorton was asked to investigate, and he organized an expedition that excavated the strange remains. The archaeologists found a fishing village dating from the ninth century B.C., which had apparently been submerged in the lake bottom as the result of some violent natural catastrophe. Thousands of clay vessels and pieces of stoneware were scattered over the area, and row upon row of houses, or parts of their remains, were found imbedded in the lake bottom. The village had been inhabited by a simple people who lived in the region of central Italy long before the city of Rome was built, and this was the first time their houses and other personal goods had ever been found in large quantities.

The Mystery of Atlantis

According to legend, there was once a great island nation named "Atlantis," which was inhabited by a cultured and sophisticated people whose achievements in art and science were the envy of the civilized world. Suddenly, Atlantis disappeared without a trace, apparently swallowed up by the sea. Ever since, archaeologists and historians have dreamed of finding this "lost continent"—as it has often been called—and unravelling the mystery of its ancient and intriguing legend.

In the last century, scholars and scientists have advanced many theories to explain the legend of Atlantis, but probably the most likely explanation is that the place

the ancients called Atlantis was the Greek island now called "Santorini." Research has revealed that Santorini was once inhabited by a highly developed and civilized culture. Excavations both on land and under water—using some of the latest scientific equipment—have produced pottery, works of art, and the remains of buildings, all dating from before 1500 B.C. This is 1,000 years before the development of the ancient Greek society with which we are familiar.

Shortly after 1500 B.C., Santorini exploded in one of the most violent volcanic eruptions known to science. The entire center portion of the island blew sky-high, leaving nothing but a gigantic crater. This crater is now a bay several miles wide, and the remainder of the island is shaped roughly like a ring. The inner edge of the ring, forming the inner walls of the crater, is a sheer cliff several hundred feet high. The outer edge slopes gently down to the sea, and the shores of Santorini are ringed with miles and miles of black volcanic sand.

Whether Santorini was, in fact, the civilization of Atlantis is a question we may never be able to answer to everyone's satisfaction. But the remains of a sunken city are there, and there is no doubt either that its people were advanced in art and science or that this city was suddenly destroyed and cast into the sea. Remains such as those of Santorini or of Herod's magnificent harbor at Caesarea show that ancient legends may be closer to the truth than our skeptical modern world is sometimes willing to admit.

VI THE FUTURE OF UNDERWATER ARCHAEOLOGY

Underwater archaeology is a young science, but it is rapidly coming of age. In the beginning, archaeologists were thankful for any object that could be recovered from the sea bottom. Now they demand that underwater excavations be carried out carefully and precisely so that, as underwater remains are removed from the sea, as much information as possible is preserved. In the past, the accidental discoveries of local divers and fishermen have led archaeologists to some of their richest and most valuable finds, but they will not be able to depend on this source of information forever. Eventually, underwater archaeologists must come to rely almost completely on their own techniques in order to locate and explore the many underwater sites that are so well covered or in such deep water that they will never be visible to the diver or fisherman who accidentally happens to pass by.

In past years, underwater archae-ologists have concentrated on investigating the remains of ancient civilizations that the nations of the modern western world consider most interesting and know the most about. The Phoenicians, Greeks, Romans, and Byzantines are those who have been most favored over other seafaring nations of ancient times. Yet the Egyptians, the Minoans, the coastal peoples of Syria and Asia Minor, and the pre-Classical Greeks were also important seafarers, as were many of the ancient peoples of the Indian Ocean, the China Sea, and the Western Pacific.

There are probably more gaps in our knowledge of seafaring than there are places filled in. Archaeologists have barely begun the immense task of gathering together and organizing the wealth of information from the sciences of oceanography, geology, geography, history, and marine biology, all of which have something to contribute to our knowledge of the history of seafaring.

This diver is photographing the Yassi Ada shipwreck with a special stereoscopic camera that produces a three-dimensional picture.

The hull of the Yassi Ada wreck. The careful scientific excavation of this ancient shipwreck was one of the most important projects undertaken by modern underwater archaeologists.

For those of you who love the sea, who crave the excitement and adventure of underwater work, and who are fascinated by the scientific and historical information that lies on the bottom of the seas and oceans, underwater archaeology could be an exciting and rewarding profession. Fortunately for those who might want to become underwater archaeologists, the work of this young science has only just begun!

GLOSSARY

air compressor	A motor-driven device that pumps air into a tank
air lift	A kind of suction hose used to excavate underwater ruins. Air from an air compressor is pumped through the hose from the bottom, causing a suction that draws up mud and sand from the ocean floor. A filter at the top of the hose catches small artifacts drawn into the air lift.
amphora	A two-handled pottery vessel, used to hold wine, oil, or other liquids.
aqualung	An underwater breathing apparatus using a tank of compressed air and a regulator through which the diver breathes.
barnacle	A small sea animal that attaches its hard shell to a submerged surface
compressed-air tank	A metal tank designed to hold air under pressure, used in underwater breathing equipment
coral	Tiny sea animals that live in colonies, forming a rock-like mass as new layers of shell material are added with each new generation
coral reef	An underwater mound built up of coral and the remains of sea life
cubmarine	A small research submarine used for underwater survey work
grappling hook	A metal shaft with claws at one end, used for grasping and holding large objects

hydrodynamic cradle	A device for towing divers under water
marking buoy	A float used for marking the location of some object that lies below the surface
mosaic	A picture or design made up of many small pieces arranged in a certain pattern
plexiglass	A hard, transparent plastic sheet used as window material
proton magnetometer	An electronic device that can detect metal objects at great distances under water
sand bar	A large, long mound of sand deposited on the bottom of a body of water by the action of waves or currents
sea wall	A massive wall built up from the sea floor and rising above the surface of the water, designed to protect a harbor from the destructive force of waves and currents
side-scan sonar	An improved form of sonar using a wide-angle beam to survey a larger area of the sea floor
sonar	An electronic device using sound waves to determine the contours of the sea floor and to indicate the presence of buried artifacts.
towvane	A device that allows a diver either to be lowered straight down or towed along under water

INDEX

ACKNOWLEDGMENTS

The illustrations are reproduced through the courtesly of: Under Sea Exploration Society, Israel P. 8; 11–13; 19; 21–23; 26; 28; 33–36; 53; 58–61; 69; 70; 72; 77; 84; 85. Peter Throckmorton P. 10; 45; 46; 49; 91; 92. Israel Exploration Journal P. 16; National Museum, Athens P. 41; Alinari P. 43. Drawing by H. Maggi P. 47. John Veltri P. 51. David Owen P. 55. Vikingeskibshallen i Roskilde P. 62. The Maritime Museum and the Warship Wasa P. 65. From Wittacker Oceanography, Wormley, Surrey P. 79. Drawing by Curt Scott P. 80. Maritime Museum, Haifa P. 82. Haifa University, Center for Maritime Studies P. 86.

ELISHA LINDER is a lecturer in ancient seafaring at the University of Haifa's Center for Maritime Studies. He also holds the position of research fellow in maritime archaeology at the Hebrew University in Jerusalem. Dr Linder received his M.A. from Columbia University, New York, and his Ph.D. from Brandeis University in Massachusetts. During his career as a marine archaeologist in Israel, he has directed expeditions at sites such as Acco, Atlit, and Ashdod. Dr. Linder is the author of several studies dealing with maritime history and archaeology.

AVNER RABAN, who lectures in the Department of Maritime Studies at the University of Haifa, is also a practicing marine archaeologist. He has organized underwater explorations in Cyprus and in Israel.

RICHARD L. CURRIER received his A.B. and Ph.D. degrees in anthropology from the University of California at Berkeley. He has done field work in Mexico and in Greece and has taught anthropology both at Berkeley and at the University of Minnesota. Dr. Currier now devotes full time to writing and research.